Denmark Travel Guide 2023-2024

Explore Denmark's Abundant Heritage, Culture, Magnificent Landscapes, Lifestyle, and Delicious Dishes in this 2023-2024 Travel Guide!

(Road map travel guide to Denmark)

Rawlings Scott

Denmark Road map

Abstract

Explore the captivating beauty of Denmark with our comprehensive travel guide. Delve into the country's rich history, culture, and natural wonders. From the bustling city of Copenhagen to the quaint towns of Aarhus and Odense, uncover the unique attractions and hidden gems each destination has to offer.

Discover the splendor of Danish nature through its national parks, coastal areas, and picturesque islands.

Sample the delicious Danish cuisine, savoring traditional dishes and mouth-watering pastries. Immerse yourself in the world of Danish arts and design, from innovative architecture to captivating museums.

Gain insight into local customs and etiquette to enhance your cultural experience. Our guide also provides practical tips, safety advice, and useful phrases to ensure a smooth and unforgettable journey. Embark on a remarkable adventure as you explore the wonders of Denmark, creating memories that will last a lifetime.

Table of content

Introduction To Denmark travel guide

Welcome to our comprehensive travel guide to Denmark, a captivating country situated in the middle of Scandinavia. With its long history, lively cities, stunning scenery, and unique cultural offerings, Denmark provides a truly remarkable experience for every traveler. Whether you're exploring the picturesque canals of Copenhagen, discovering the Viking heritage in Roskilde, or immersing yourself in the serenity of Danish nature, this guide is your portal to uncovering the best of what Denmark has to offer. From useful information and insider advice to must-see attractions and hidden gems, let us be your reliable companion as you embark on an extraordinary journey through the land of the Dane

Chapter one

Introduction to Denmark

Overview of Denmark

Denmark, officially known as the Kingdom of Denmark, is a Nordic country located in Northern Europe. It is the southernmost of the Scandinavian countries and is bordered by Germany to the south. This article provides an overview of Denmark, including its geography and climate, history and culture, and practical information for visitors.

Denmark is mainly composed of the Jutland Peninsula and several islands, the largest of which are Zealand, Funen, and Bornholm. The country is known for its flat landscape, with gently rolling hills and fertile plains, as well as its extensive coastline, which is about 7,300 kilometers long and is lined with beautiful sandy beaches and quaint fishing villages.

Geography and Climate

The climate in Denmark is temperate and maritime, with mild winters and cool summers. The country experiences frequent weather changes, with precipitation occurring throughout the year. The average temperature in winter is between 0°C and 4°C (32°F and 39°F), while in summer, it ranges from 15°C to 25°C (59°F to 77°F). Denmark's weather is moderated by the warm Gulf Stream.

History and Culture

Denmark has a long and interesting history that dates back thousands of years. The country was once inhabited by the Vikings during the Viking Age, and their legacy is still evident in Danish culture today. Denmark was once a powerful kingdom and played a significant role in European history. In the 19th century, it transitioned into a constitutional monarchy, which it remains today.

Danish culture is known for its focus on equality, social welfare, and environmental sustainability. The Danish people are known for their friendliness, hospitality, and a strong sense of community.

The concept of "hygge" is deeply ingrained in Danish culture, representing a cozy and comfortable lifestyle. Denmark is also renowned for its design, architecture, and contributions to the arts, including renowned figures like Hans Christian Andersen and the iconic architect Jørn Utzon.

Practical Information

Traveling to Denmark is relatively easy, as the country has a well-developed transportation system. Copenhagen, the capital city, is served by an international airport, which offers connections to major cities worldwide. Denmark has an extensive network of trains, buses, and ferries, making it convenient to explore different regions of the country.

The official language in Denmark is Danish, but English is widely spoken, especially in tourist areas. The currency is the Danish Krone (DKK), and credit cards are widely accepted. Denmark has a high standard of living, and the cost of living can be relatively high compared to other European countries.

When it comes to accommodation, Denmark offers a range of options, including hotels, guesthouses, and vacation rentals. The country has a diverse culinary scene, and visitors can enjoy traditional Danish cuisine, which often features seafood, pork, and dairy products.

In terms of attractions, Denmark has much to offer.

Copenhagen, with its charming canals, historic sites like the Amalienborg Palace and Rosenborg Castle, and the iconic Little Mermaid statue, is a must-see. Other notable destinations include the colorful waterfront of Nyhavn, the ancient city of Aarhus, and the fairy-tale-like castles of North Zealand. Visitors from European Union countries can use the European Health Insurance Card (EHIC) for emergency medical treatment, while non-EU visitors are advised to have travel insurance to cover any healthcare expenses.

Chapter two

Plan your trip to Denmark

There are several important factors to consider when planning your trip to Denmark. This comprehensive guide covers when to travel to Denmark, visa and entry requirements, transportation options, how to get to Denmark, domestic travel, accommodation options, currency and money issues, language and communication, and the importance of travel insurance. Provides important information about.

When is the best time to visit Denmark?

Denmark has a temperate maritime climate, with mild and relatively cool weather all year round. The best time to go to Denmark depends a lot on your preferences and what activities you want to do during your trip.

Summer (June to August) is the peak tourist season in Denmark, with average temperatures ranging from 15°C to 25°C (59°F to 77°F). The long hours of sunshine give you plenty of time to explore the country's many attractions, enjoy outdoor activities and enjoy the vibrant summer festivals.

Spring (April-May) and autumn (September-October) are also pleasant seasons to visit Denmark. The weather is generally mild during this period, and you can enjoy beautiful flowers in spring and colorful leaves in autumn. The low season offers a quieter and cheaper experience compared to summer.

Danish winters (December to February) are cold with temperatures ranging from 0°C to 4°C (32°F to 39°F). However, if you don't mind cold weather, winter is a great time to visit, especially during the holiday season. The country is adorned with festive decorations and you can experience the best of Danish 'Hygge' concepts: cozy cafes, Christmas markets, and traditional holiday celebrations.

Denmark visa and entry requirements

Denmark is a member of the Schengen Area and citizens of many countries can travel visa-free for short stays of up to 90 days within 180 days. However, visa requirements vary by nationality. It is important to check visa requirements well in advance of travel to ensure compliance. If you are a national of a country that requires a visa to enter Denmark, you must apply for a Schengen visa at the Danish Embassy or Consulate in your home country. The application process typically involves submitting required documents such as B. A valid passport, proof of accommodation, itinerary, travel insurance, and proof of funds for your stay.

It is important to note that visa requirements are subject to change. Therefore, we recommend that you contact the Danish embassy or consulate in your home country or visit the official website of the Danish Immigration Service for up-to-date information

Transportation

Arrive in Denmark

Denmark is easily accessible by air, land, and sea. Copenhagen Airport (Kastrup) is the country's largest international airport and serves as a major gateway for travelers. With direct flights to major cities around the world, you can easily reach Denmark from almost anywhere. International flights are also available at other Danish airports such as Billund and Aalborg airports.

If you prefer to travel by land, Denmark has well-developed roads with neighboring countries.
Denmark can be reached by car or bus via Europe's extensive road network. The öresund Bridge, which connects Denmark and Sweden, is a notable landmark and provides a convenient link between the two countries. You can also reach Denmark by ferry, especially if you come from neighboring countries such as Germany or Sweden.
Several ferry services operate between Denmark and various destinations, including the popular route between Copenhagen and Oslo, Norway.

Getting around Denmark

Once you've arrived in Denmark, you have a wide range of transport options to get around the country.
Public transport in Denmark is efficient and well-connected. train, The main means of public transport in Denmark are buses and ferries.

The national rail network, operated by DSB (Danish State Railways), covers most of Denmark's larger towns and cities, providing comfortable and reliable rail connections.

The trains are equipped with the latest equipment and you can enjoy beautiful views of the countryside as you travel. Buses are a great option for trips within cities and to remote areas where trains do not go. Denmark's bus network is extensive, with local bus companies providing regular connections to various destinations. Copenhagen, in particular, has an efficient bus system that connects various parts of the city and outskirts.

Since Denmark has many islands, ferries are an essential means of transportation. Ferries run between the mainland and islands such as Geelan, Funen, and Bornholm, making it a convenient way to explore these unique destinations.

The ferries are well-maintained and offer great views of the Danish coast during the journey.

Cycling is very popular in Denmark and the country has an extensive network of well-maintained cycle paths. Renting a bike is a great way to explore cities and towns at your own pace, and lets you experience Denmark's commitment to sustainability and green transport.

For those who value driving convenience, a rental car is a viable option. Denmark has excellent road infrastructure and driving within the country is generally safe and easy.

However, be aware that parking in urban areas is limited and can be expensive. Therefore, it is recommended to check the availability of parking in advance.

Accommodation options

Denmark offers a wide range of accommodation options for different budgets and tastes. Suitable accommodations can be found all over the country, including luxury hotels, cozy guesthouses, and budget hostels.

In big cities like Copenhagen, Aarhus, and Odense, you'll find a wide range of hotels, from luxury hotels to boutique hotels to budget chains.

These hotels offer conveniences such as Wi-Fi, breakfast, and in some cases additional facilities such as fitness centers and spa services. For a more local experience, consider staying in a guest house or bed and breakfast (B&B). These accommodations offer a cozy and intimate atmosphere, often with personal service and the opportunity to connect with local hosts. Our guesthouses are located both in the city and in the countryside, so you can experience Danish hospitality in a variety of settings.

Hostels are an affordable option, especially for budget travelers and those looking for a social atmosphere.

Denmark has several hostels offering dormitory-style rooms and shared facilities, especially in popular tourist destinations. Hostels are a great way to meet other travelers and share experiences.

In addition, villas are becoming more and more popular in Denmark. Websites and platforms like Airbnb and HomeAway offer a wide range of apartments, homes, and vacation homes for short-term rental. Vacation rentals are especially good for families and groups of friends as they offer more space and the ability to self-care.
currency and money issues

The Danish currency is the Danish Krone (DKK). Cash is widely accepted in Denmark and most cities have ATMs that allow you to withdraw Danish kroner with your debit or credit card. Credit and debit cards are widely accepted in shops, restaurants, and hotels, so there's no need to carry cash.

We recommend that you inform your bank or credit card company of your travel plans to ensure that you can use your card during your stay in Denmark.

Some banks may charge a fee for foreign transactions, so you should check with your bank for additional fees that may apply.

Language and communication

The official language in Denmark is Danish, but English is widely used and understood, especially in tourist areas, hotels, restaurants, and shops. You will have no trouble communicating in English while visiting Denmark.

The pronunciation and vocabulary of Danish may differ from that of English, but most Danes have a good level of English and are usually happy to help if they need help or guidance. Denmark is consistently ranked among the best countries in the world for English proficiency. If you want to immerse yourself in the local culture and make a good impression, learning some basic Danish phrases can be appreciated by the locals. Simple greetings like "Hej" (Hello), "Tak" (Thank you), and "Undskyld" (Sorry) can be of great help in establishing a friendly connection.

Travel Insurance

Having travel insurance is highly recommended when visiting Denmark or any other destination. Travel insurance provides coverage for unforeseen circumstances such as medical emergencies, canceled or interrupted trips, lost or stolen belongings, and liability issues.

Before purchasing travel insurance, review the policy carefully to make sure it meets your specific needs. Check to see if it includes health insurance, especially if you are not eligible for urgent health care under the European Health Insurance Card (EHIC).

Review coverage limits, deductibles, and exclusions, and be aware of any pre-existing medical conditions that may affect coverage.

You must carry a copy of your travel insurance policy and emergency phone numbers when you travel. Familiarize yourself with the claims process and keep all necessary documents, receipts, and medical records in case you need to file a claim.

Conclusion

Planning a trip to Denmark involves considering various factors such as the ideal time to visit, visa requirements, transportation options, accommodation options, financial issues key, language and communication as well as the importance of travel insurance.

By considering these aspects and taking the necessary preparations, you can ensure an enjoyable visit to this charming Nordic country.

Denmark's rich history, vibrant culture, beautiful scenery, and friendly people are sure to leave you with unforgettable memories during your trip.

Chapter three

Explore Copenhagen:

An Overview of the Capital of Denmark

Copenhagen, the capital of Denmark, is a vibrant and charming metropolis known for its rich history, innovative design, beautiful canals, and world-class cuisine. This article provides a comprehensive overview of Copenhagen and highlights popular attractions such as Tivoli Gardens, The Little Mermaid, Nyhavn, museums and galleries, parks and gardens, and the city's shopping, dining, nightlife, and entertainment venues. to introduce.

Overview of Copenhagen

Copenhagen, located on the east coast of Zealand Island, is a cultural and economic center with a population of about 800,000. A seamless blend of historic heritage and modern innovation, the city offers a unique blend of old-world charm and contemporary design.

Copenhagen's architecture is a testament to its rich history. Medieval buildings, Renaissance castles, and 18th-century mansions blend harmoniously with elegant modern architecture. The city's commitment to sustainability is evident in its bike-friendly infrastructure, efficient public transport, and green spaces.

Top Landmarks in Copenhagen

1. Tivoli Gardens:
Tivoli Gardens is a must-see attraction in Copenhagen. Established in 1843, this historic amusement park offers a magical experience for visitors of all ages. Beautiful gardens, enchanting rides, live performances, and a festive atmosphere make Tivoli Gardens a true Copenhagen icon. 2. Little Mermaid Statue:
Inspired by Hans Christian Andersen's famous fairy tale, the Little Mermaid statue is an iconic symbol of Copenhagen. Located on the Langelinie promenade, this small but important sculpture attracts millions of visitors each year.

3.Nyhavn:

Nyhavn is a quaint waterfront district known for its colorful 17th and 18th-century townhouses, lively atmosphere, and charming cafes and restaurants. Take a stroll along the canals, enjoy a boat tour, or just relax with a drink by the water.

4. Museums and galleries:

Copenhagen is full of museums and galleries that showcase its rich cultural heritage. The National Museum, the New York Carlsberg Glyptotec, and the Louisiana Museum of Modern Art are just a few of the city's excellent cultural venues.

5. Parks and Gardens:

Copenhagen is known for its abundance of green spaces. King's Garden is next to Rosenborg Castle and is a popular place for picnics and leisurely walks. The Botanical Gardens are a nature lover's paradise with a

wide variety of plants, and Faled Parken hosts fun activities and open-air concerts.

Shopping and dining in Copenhagen

Copenhagen is a shopper's paradise with a wide range of shopping streets and boutiques to suit every taste and budget. One of Europe's longest pedestrian streets, Strøget is lined with quality fashion brands, international retailers, and Danish design shops. Go shopping or explore the vibrant Vesterbro district, known for its independent boutiques and trendy shops. Equally impressive is the city's gastronomic scene, which combines traditional Danish cuisine with innovative gastronomy.

From Michelin-starred restaurants to trendy food markets, Copenhagen's food landscape is a gourmand's delight. Don't miss the chance to sample sombreros (open-faced sandwiches), Danish pastries, and famous New Nordic dishes at famous places such as Norma.

nightlife and entertainment

Copenhagen comes to life after dark, offering a vibrant nightlife for everyone. The city has many bars, clubs, live music venues, and theaters, catering to all tastes and tastes. Visit the trendy Vesterbro district with its hip bars and clubs, or explore the multicultural district of Noahbro, known for its diverse nightlife.

The Meatpacking District in the Vesterbro district has transformed old slaughterhouses into trendy bars and restaurants, making it a popular nightlife destination. For live music lovers, Vega and The Pumpehusett is a renowned venue that hosts national and international artists of various genres. The Royal Danish Opera and Royal Danish Theater offer world-class performances including ballets, operas, and theatrical productions.

actionable information

For a unique and immersive experience, consider visiting Tivoli Gardens in the evening. Illuminated rides, live music, and dazzling fireworks transform the park into a magical wonderland.

Copenhagen's vibrant LGBTQ+ scene is also worth exploring. Known for its inclusive atmosphere, the city hosts the annual Copenhagen Pride, a colorful celebration of diversity and equality.

1. Movement:
Copenhagen has an excellent public transport system with buses, trains, and an extensive metro network. The city's efficient bike-sharing program and pedestrian-friendly roads make biking and walking popular modes of transportation.

2. weather:
Copenhagen has a temperate maritime climate. Summers are generally mild with temperatures between 15°C and 25°C (59°F and 77°F). Winters are cold, with temperatures ranging from 0°C to 4°C (32°F to 39°F). It is recommended to check the

weather forecast before visiting and prepare accordingly.

3. language:

Denmark's official language is Danish, but English is widely spoken and understood in Copenhagen. I had no problem communicating in English during my stay.

4. Currency:

The Danish currency is the Danish Krone (DKK). Most stores accept major credit cards, but it's a good idea to always have cash on hand for small purchases and visits to local markets.

5. Security:

Copenhagen is generally a safe city for travelers. However, we recommend that you always take the usual precautions.

B. Watch your belongings, avoid unlit and secluded areas at night, and be aware of your surroundings.

In summary, Copenhagen has a lot to offer, from historic landmarks to modern wonders, making it an ideal destination for travelers. A unique blend of culture, design, gastronomy, and vibrant nightlife, the Danish capital captivates visitors with its charm and character. Whether exploring the famous Tivoli Gardens, admiring the Little Mermaid statue, strolling through picturesque Nyhavn, immersing yourself in art and culture, shopping, and dining, Copenhagen has something for everyone. We promise you an unforgettable experience.

Chapter four

Discover other Danish cities in Denmark

Copenhagen is perhaps Denmark's most famous city, but several other captivating cities offer unique cultural experiences, historical attractions, and natural beauty. In this article, we'll take a look at some of these cities, each with its character and charm, including Aarhus, Odense, Aalborg, Roskilde, Helsingor, Ribe, and Vyborg.

1. Aarhus:
Located on the east coast of Jutland, Aarhus is Denmark's second-largest city and a vibrant cultural center. The city seamlessly blends its rich history with contemporary architecture and a thriving arts scene. A must-see is the ARoS Aarhus Art Museum, known for its contemporary art exhibits and

the iconic Rainbow Panorama, a circular walkway offering panoramic views of the city. Wander the quaint cobbled streets of the Latin Quarter, visit the historic Aarhus Cathedral, and stroll along the beautiful Aarhus Harbour. Aarhus is also home to beautiful beaches, such as Bellevue Beach, where you can relax and enjoy the coastal views.

2. Odense:

Known as the birthplace of the famous fairy tale writer Hans, his Christian Andersen, Odense is a charming city on the island of Funen. Immerse yourself in the world of Andersen at the Andersen Museum, where you can gain insight into his life and work.

Explore the quaint old town with half-timbered houses, visit Odense Cathedral, and stroll through the enchanting gardens of Funen village, an open-air museum that showcases life in the Danish countryside. Odense also has several parks and green spaces perfect for leisurely walks and picnics, including beautiful Kongenshave.

3. Aalborg:
Located in North Jutland, Aalborg is a vibrant city with a rich Viking history. Explore the Viking Cemetery of Lindholm Hoye and the historic Aalborg Castle.

Visit the Aalborg Historical Museum to learn about the city's history, and stroll through the lively John Fleuane gate, a bustling street lined with restaurants, bars, and live music venues. Aalborg is also home to cultural attractions such as the Aalborg Symphony Orchestra and the Utzon Center, a museum dedicated to the works of the famous Danish architect Jorn Utzon. Aalborg Zoo is a must-visit. A variety of animal species are housed, providing an educational experience for visitors of all ages.

4. Roskilde:

Located on the island of Zealand, Roskilde is a historic town with some significant cultural heritage. A highlight of Roskilde is Roskilde Cathedral, a UNESCO World Heritage Site.

A masterpiece of Gothic architecture, it is the burial place of the Danish king and his queen. The Viking Ship Museum offers an interesting insight into the Viking Age, showcases restored Viking ships, and offers an interactive experience. Roskilde is also known for the annual Roskilde Festival, one of Europe's largest music festivals, attracting international artists and music lovers from all over the world.

5. Helsingor

Located on the northeastern tip of Zealand, Helsingor is a picturesque seaside town known for its impressive Kronborg Castle, known as Helsingor in Shakespeare's Hamlet. Explore the castle's great halls, visit the Danish Maritime Museum, and enjoy panoramic views of the Öresund Strait.

Wander the charming streets of Old Town Elsinore, lined with historic buildings and

quaint shops. From Helsingor you can also take a ferry to the Swedish city of Helsingborg, giving him a unique opportunity to explore two countries in one trip.

6. Ribe:
Denmark's oldest town, Ribe is a living time capsule with well-preserved medieval architecture and cobbled streets. Wander the narrow streets of the Old Town and admire the charming half-timbered houses.
Visit Ribe Cathedral, one of Denmark's most magnificent Romanesque churches, and explore the Ribe Viking Center, an open-air museum that recreates Viking life.

Take a boat trip on the River Ribe or join a guided walking tour to learn about the city's fascinating history. Ribe is also the gateway to the nearby Wadden Sea National Park, a UNESCO World Heritage Site and an important habitat for migratory birds and marine life.

7. Vyborg:

Located in central Jutland, Vyborg is a historic city with a rich cultural heritage. The twin-towered Viborg Cathedral is an impressive landmark and it is one of Denmark's most important Romanesque churches.

Stroll through the charming streets of the Old Town, visit the Viborg Museum to learn about the city's history, and enjoy the tranquility of Hartsee with its beautiful nature trails and scenic views. Viborg is also known for its annual Viborg Animation Festival. The festival screens animated films from around the world and brings together animation enthusiasts and professionals alike.

Each of these Danish cities offers a unique blend of history, culture, and natural beauty, giving visitors a deeper understanding of Denmark's diverse heritage. Explore Aarhus' contemporary art scene, discover Odense's fairytale heritage, soak up Viking history in Aalborg, experience the medieval charm of Ribe, and marvel at the wonders of Kronborg Castle in Elsinore. Then you will surely be fascinated. A rich tapestry of these cities.

Practical information:
Getting around:
Public transportation such as buses and trains is widely available in these cities. Cycling is also a popular and convenient option, and most cities have designated bike lanes. hotel:
Each city has a range of accommodation options, from budget hostels to luxury hotels. It is advisable to book in advance, especially during peak travel seasons.

eat:

Taste local and international cuisine at the many restaurants, cafes, and street food stalls in these cities. Don't miss the chance to try traditional Danish dishes such as smorrebrod (open sandwiches) and elusive (round pancakes).

Festivals and Events:

Check the local events calendar for festivals, cultural events, and concerts taking place during your stay. These cities host a variety of festivals throughout the year that give a sense of local tradition and vibrancy.

Chapter five

Exploring Danish Nature in Denmark

National Parks

Coastal Areas and Beaches

Denmark is known for its charming cities and rich cultural heritage, but it also offers a wealth of natural beauty and outdoor adventures. From pristine national parks to beautiful coastal areas, picturesque islands, lush forests, and tranquil lakes, Denmark has something to offer nature lovers and outdoor adventurers. In this article, we'll take a look at the different landscapes and outdoor activities that await you in Denmark.

National park:

Denmark has some amazing national parks that showcase the country's natural diversity. These parks preserve unique ecosystems and wildlife habitats and offer opportunities for hiking, birdwatching, and exploration. Here are some notable national parks.

1. Thy National Park:
Thy National Park is located in the northwest of Jutland and is Denmark's first national park. It includes vast heathlands, dunes, forests, and pristine beaches. Explore the trails that wind through the park, spot rare birdlife, and experience the pristine beauty of this pristine natural gem.

2. Wadden Sea National Park:
A UNESCO World Heritage Site, the Wadden Sea National Park stretches along Denmark's west coast. This unique tidal flat features shifting sands, tidal flats, and abundant birdlife. Take a guided tour, go on a mudflat walk, or go on a seal safari to see the region's diverse marine and bird life.

3. Mols Bjerge National Park:
Mols-Bjerge National Park is located on the DJurslsland peninsula and features rolling hills, lush forests, and scenic coastal landscapes. Hike the park's marked trails, enjoy panoramic views from the hills, and explore idyllic beaches and coastal coves.

Coastal areas and beaches:

With more than 7,300 kilometers of coastline, Denmark has abundant coastal areas and beautiful sandy beaches. Whether it's relaxation, water sports, or beautiful walks along the coast, the Danish coast has something for everyone. Here are some notable coastal destinations.

1. Skagen:
Skagen is located in the northernmost part of Denmark and is known for its amazing natural beauty. The meeting of the Skagerrak and Kattegat seas gives rise to a unique phenomenon known as the "collision of the two seas".

Visit Grenen, where you can stand with one foot on any sea, and explore the beautiful dunes and pristine beaches that surround the area.

2. Bornholm:

Located in the Baltic Sea, Bornholm is Denmark's easternmost island and a popular destination for beach lovers. Its rugged coast is dotted with beautiful sandy beaches and quaint fishing villages. Visit Duodde Beach, known for its fine white sand and crystal clear water, or explore the dramatic rock formations and sea cliffs of Hammerknuden.

Danish islands:

Denmark is made up of numerous islands, each with its own unique character and natural wonders. These islands offer a peaceful retreat from the mainland and offer opportunities for outdoor activities and exploration. Here are some famous Danish islands you should visit.

1. Funen:
Known as the 'Garden of Denmark', Funen is Denmark's third largest island and is a charming mix of countryside, coastal scenery, and historic sites. Explore the picturesque scenery of the Funen 'Alps' in Bakker, visit the romantic Egeskov Castle, or relax in the idyllic coastal towns of Svenndborg and Forborg. Uka

2. Leso:

Located in the Kattegat Sea, Leso is a tranquil island known for its beautiful beaches, moors, and traditional thatched houses. Immerse yourself in the island's unique culture, visit the Leso salt fields to learn about the island's salt-making traditions, or cycle through the beautiful countryside.

3. Zealand:

Denmark's largest island, Zealand, is home to the capital, Copenhagen, and diverse natural landscapes. Explore the stunning cliffs and sandy beaches of Mons Klint, or visit the tranquil island of Samsoe, known for its renewable energy efforts and beautiful scenery.

Zealand also has charming coastal towns such as Girleye and Hornbeck, where you can relax on beautiful beaches and enjoy fresh seafood.

Forest and lake:

Denmark may not be known for its extensive forests, but it still has quiet woodlands and calm lakes perfect for nature lovers. Here are some destinations that will immerse you in the tranquility of Danish forests and lakes.

1. Lake Silkeborg:
Located in central Jutland, the Silkeborg Lakes consist of a series of interconnected lakes surrounded by lush forests.

Rent a canoe or kayak and explore the area by paddling the calm waters and enjoying the beautiful surroundings. Hiking and biking trails also pass through the area, allowing you to discover hidden gems along the lakeshore.

2. Grybskov Forest:
The Grybskov Forest is located in northern New Zealand and is one of Denmark's largest and most beautiful forests. This ancient forest is home to diverse flora and fauna, and there are many hiking trails to explore. Discover enchanting lakes, historic sites, and secluded picnic areas as you hike through the forest.

Denmark's natural landscape offers many opportunities for outdoor activities and adventures. Hiking, biking, kayaking, wildlife viewing, and many other activities are available. Here are some popular outdoor activities in Denmark.

1. Cycling:
Known for its extensive network of bike paths, Denmark is a paradise for cyclists. Rent a bike and explore the beautiful countryside, quaint villages, and coastal trails at your own pace.

2. Hiking:
Lace up your hiking boots and embark on a scenic hike through Denmark's national parks, coastal regions, and forests.

The country offers a variety of marked trails suitable for hikers of all levels.

3. Birdwatching:
Denmark is a birdwatcher's paradise as its numerous coastal areas, wetlands, and nature reserves attract a wide variety of bird species. Visit the Skagen Bird Observatory or the Wadd
en Sea National Park for some great birdwatching.

4. Water sports:
With its extensive coastline and calm seas, Denmark is a great destination for water sports enthusiasts. Try kayaking, paddling, windsurfing, and kitesurfing along the coast.

Always remember to respect nature and follow the guidelines and restrictions that apply to protect the natural environment.

In summary, Denmark's natural beauty extends beyond its charming cities, offering nature lovers a wide choice of landscapes and outdoor activities. From national parks and coastal areas to picturesque islands, forests, and lakes, Denmark offers many opportunities to explore and reconnect with nature. Whether hiking through beautiful national parks, relaxing on sandy beaches, exploring unique islands, hiking through tranquil forests, or engaging in outdoor activities, Denmark's natural wonders are an unforgettable experience. And it will bring you a deep appreciation for the diversity and nature of this country. enchanting landscape.

Chapter six

Danish Cuisine and Beverages: Traditional Dishes,
Local Ingredients, Pastries, and Beverages

Denmark may not be as internationally known for its cuisine as other European countries, but it has a rich culinary tradition that reflects the country's history, geography, and cultural traditions. Danish cuisine is known for its simplicity, with an emphasis on local and seasonal ingredients, and delicious pastries that are synonymous with Danish culture. This article covers traditional Danish food, local ingredients, culinary traditions, Danish pastries and desserts, Danish beer, and aquavit.

1. Smorrebrod

A smorrebrod is an iconic Danish sandwich made from a slice of rye bread topped with a variety of ingredients such as herring, liver pate, smoked salmon, and roast beef. These sandwiches are often beautifully topped with fresh herbs, pickles, and onions.

2. Frikadeller

Frikadeller are Danish meatballs made with pork and beef, onions, eggs, bread crumbs, and spices. It is usually served with potatoes, gravy, and pickled red cabbage.

3. Stegt flask with Persilesov:

This classic Danish dish consists of boiled potatoes served with slices of fried pork belly and a creamy parsley sauce.

The pork belly is crispy on the outside and soft on the inside, creating a delicious combination of flavors and textures.

4. Able Flask:
Able Flask is a traditional Danish dish that combines crispy fried bacon with caramelized apple slices. The combination of umami and sweetness creates a unique taste.

5. Lever postej:
Leverpostej is a folie gras pie made with pork liver, onions, butter, and spices. It is often spread on rye bread and topped with pickles or bacon.

Danish cuisine places great emphasis on local and seasonal ingredients. The country's agricultural traditions and the availability of fresh produce and seafood have shaped the food landscape. The main ingredients and culinary traditions include:

1. Seafood:
With a long coastline and proximity to the sea, Denmark has a long tradition of eating seafood. Popular fish species include herring, cod, salmon, and flounder. Smoked and pickled herrings, which are often used in traditional Danish cuisine, are particularly popular.

2. potatoes:

Potatoes are a staple of Danish cuisine and are boiled, mashed, roasted, and served in many forms. They accompany many traditional dishes and give the meal a hearty and useful accent.

3. Dairy products:

Denmark is known for its high-quality dairy products such as butter, cheese, and milk. Danish butter is highly valued for its rich flavor and creamy texture. 4. Foraging:

Foraging is a popular Danish culinary tradition, with locals venturing into forests and meadows to gather wild ingredients such as mushrooms, berries, and herbs. These ingredients are often incorporated into traditional dishes and contribute to the unique flavor of Danish cuisine.

No Danish culinary quest is complete without mentioning the world-famous Danish pastry, also known as Wienerbrot. These buttery, crunchy flavors are synonymous with Danish food culture. Popular Danish baked goods include:

1. Kanelbullar (cinnamon rolls):
Cinnamon rolls are a popular Danish pastry, often eaten for breakfast or as a sweet treat throughout the day. The dough is usually topped with a mixture of butter, sugar, and cinnamon, and is then topped with frosting.

2. Hindbear Snitter:
Hindbernitters are rectangular pastries filled with raspberry jam and topped with icing.

3. Smorrebrod and Danish Beer and Aquavit:

Besides pastries and desserts, Denmark is also known for beer and aquavit, a traditional Scandinavian spirit. Beer in Denmark has a rich history and the country has a thriving craft beer scene. Popular Danish beers include:

1. Carlsberg: Carlsberg is one of Denmark's most renowned brew brands, known for its fresh and invigorating ales. It has a well-established history and is broadly delighted both locally and universally.

2. Mikkeller: Mikkeller is a famous Danish art brewery that has earned worldwide respect for its creative and exploratory lagers. They produce many interesting and tasty mixes, frequently working together with different distilleries and pushing the limits of conventional brew styles.

3. Tuborg: Tuborg is another notable Danish brew brand. It offers various lagers, including ales, pilsners, and specialty blends.

Tuborg is in many cases delighted during happy events and is a well-known decision for open-air social occasions and summer parties.

Aquavit is a customary Scandinavian soul that holds an exceptional spot in Danish culture. It is commonly seasoned with spices and flavors, like caraway or dill, and delighted in as a digestif. Aquavit is in many cases served chilled in little glasses and can be tasted or delighted in as a shot. It is known for its particular flavor and is frequently matched with customary Danish dishes.

All in all, Danish food is a great mix of customary dishes, neighborhood fixings, cakes, and refreshments that mirror the country's social legacy and culinary practices. From the notorious smørrebrød and generous frikadeller to the incredibly popular Danish baked goods and a flourishing specialty brew scene, Denmark offers a large number of flavors and encounters for food and refreshment devotees. In this way, whether you're investigating the customary dishes, enjoying a heavenly Danish cake, or raising a glass of Danish lager or aquavit, you're certain to find the rich and different culinary pleasures that Denmark brings to the table

Chapter seven

*Danish Arts and Design: Danish Design and
Architecture, Art Museums and Galleries, Performing
Arts and Music, Street Art, and Urban Culture*

Denmark has a vibrant art and design scene that spans many disciplines, from design and architecture to visual arts, performing arts, and street art. Danish creativity is known for its minimalist and functional approach that combines aesthetics and functionality. This article looks at Danish design and architecture, museums and galleries, performing arts and music, and Denmark's thriving street art and urban culture scene.

Danish art and design
Danish design is known worldwide for its clean lines, simplicity, and focus on functionality. The Danish design movement was born in the mid-20th century and has left an indelible mark on the design world ever since. The main characteristics of Danish design are:

1. Functionalism:
Danish design emphasizes functionality and utility, often emphasizing simplicity and clear shapes. This design is known to be highly efficient and enrich your daily life.

2. Minimalism:
Danish design focuses on minimalism, using fewer elements and reducing unnecessary ornamentation. This minimalist approach brings calmness and simplicity to the design.

3. Use of natural materials:
Danish designers often use natural materials such as wood, leather, and stone, celebrating their natural beauty and sustainability. The use of these materials brings warmth and authenticity to the design.

4. Timeless aesthetics:
Danish design focuses on creating timeless pieces that stand up to passing trends. The design is durable and adaptable, intended to provide longevity and value.

Famous Danish designers and architects include Arne Jacobsen, Hans Wegner, Finn Juhl, and Borge Mogensen, who have had a major impact on international design.

In addition to design, Denmark is also known for its innovative and unique architecture. Danish architects have made significant contributions to modern architecture with notable works such as the Sydney Opera House by Jorn Utzon and the Louisiana Museum of Modern Art by Vilhelm Woehlert. The Copenhagen Opera House, the Royal Danish Theatre, and the Black Diamond (an extension of the Danish Royal Library) are other architectural masterpieces of the country.

Denmark has a thriving arts scene, with numerous museums and galleries showcasing different artistic styles and eras. Denmark's most famous museums and galleries are:

1. Statens Museum for Kunst:
The National Gallery of Denmark is located in Copenhagen and is the largest museum in the country. It houses a wide collection of Danish and world art, from classical masterpieces to contemporary works. 2. Louisiana Museum of Modern Art:
Located on the coast of Zealand, the Louisiana Museum of Modern Art is known for its stunning architecture and beautiful surroundings. The museum houses a diverse collection of modern and contemporary art,

including works by famous artists such as Picasso, Warhol, and Hockney.

3. ARoS Aarhus Art Museum:
His ARoS Aarhus Museum in Aarhus is one of the largest Nordic museums. The museum showcases a wide range of contemporary art installations, sculptures, and paintings, as well as special exhibitions showcasing Danish and international artists.

4. Glyptocket:
The Glyptotheket in Copenhagen is a museum with a vast collection of sculptures, paintings, and decorative arts. It houses an important collection of ancient Mediterranean art, as well as works by Danish artists such as Vilhelm Hammershoi.

Denmark has a vibrant performing arts scene with theater, dance, opera, and music. The country is home to renowned performing arts venues and festivals that showcase a wide variety of artistic expressions. Several

Notable venues and events in the Danish performing arts and music scene include:

1. Royal Danish Theater:
The Royal Danish Theater in Copenhagen is a prestigious institution that hosts the Royal Danish Ballet, the Royal Danish Opera, and the Royal Danish Theatre.

It showcases world-class ballet performances, opera productions, and plays.

2. Tivoli Garden:
Tivoli Gardens, located in the heart of Copenhagen, is not only a historic amusement park but also a venue for performances. In the summer, the park hosts many concerts, including classical, jazz, and contemporary performances.

3. Festival of Aarhus:
Aarhus Festuge is an annual arts festival held in Aarhus, Denmark's second-largest city. It is one of the largest cultural events in Northern Europe and offers a diverse program of music, theatre, dance, and visual arts, attracting local and international artists.

4. Copenhagen Jazz Festival:
The Copenhagen Jazz Festival is one of the most important jazz festivals in Europe, attracting jazz enthusiasts from all over the world. The festival takes place in various venues around Copenhagen and features performances by famous jazz musicians as well as emerging talent.

5. Roskilde Festival:
The Roskilde Festival is one of Europe's largest music festivals, known for featuring international artists of various genres. It takes place in Roskilde, just outside of Copenhagen, and offers a unique experience for music lovers. 6. Copenhagen Opera

Festival:
The Copenhagen Opera Festival celebrates the art of opera and features performances by international opera companies and emerging talent. The festival takes place at

various venues in Copenhagen, including the Copenhagen Opera House.

Street Art and Urban Culture:
Denmark's urban centers, especially Copenhagen, have a thriving street art scene and urban culture. Street art has become an integral part of the city's identity, with colorful murals adorning the facades of buildings, bridges, and public spaces. Some areas known for their vibrant street art include:

1. Meatpacking district (Kødbyen):
Located in Copenhagen's Vesterbro district, the Meatpacking District is an urban hub of creativity and culture. Its rudimentary industrial buildings act as canvases for street artists who create large-scale murals and graffiti.

2. Norrebro:
Nørrebro is a diverse and multicultural neighborhood in Copenhagen that has become a hotspot for street art. The streets are filled with colorful murals, colored art, and artwork, reflecting the vibrant and eclectic atmosphere of the neighborhood.

3. Free town Christiania:

Freetown Christiania is an autonomous neighborhood in Copenhagen known for its alternative lifestyle and countercultural values. The neighborhood is dotted with street art and graffiti, with artworks often conveying political and social messages.

4. Street art festival:

Copenhagen hosts street art festivals, such as Copenhagen Street Festival and Open Walls Festival, inviting local and international artists to create murals and installations across the city. These festivals contribute to the constant development of the urban art scene in Denmark.

Denmark's art and design scene is a dynamic and multifaceted landscape of creativity, innovation, and cultural expression of the country. Whether exploring iconic Danish design and architecture, immersing yourself in the extensive collections of museums and art galleries, attending performances at famous venues, experiencing vibrant urban culture and art on the streets, Denmark offers a wide range of art experiences that celebrate both tradition and contemporary expression.

Chapter eight

Cultural Etiquette and Customs of Denmark: Greetings and Social Etiquette, Dining Etiquette, Festivals, and Celebrations

Known for its friendly and egalitarian society, Denmark has its cultural etiquette and customs that are important to understand when visiting or interacting with Danes. This article summarizes Danish greetings, social etiquette, dining etiquette, festivals, and celebrations.

Greetings and Social Etiquette:

1. Greetings:

In Denmark, the most common form of greeting when meeting someone for the first time or in a formal setting is a handshake. Maintaining eye contact and giving a firm handshake is common.

Close friends and family may greet each other with a hug or a kiss on the cheek.

2. Punctuality:
Danes are punctual and value punctuality at social events. It is considered respectful to arrive a few minutes early or on time. If delays are expected, it is a courtesy to notify the person or organizer in advance. 3. Informality and equality:
Danish society is known for its informal and egalitarian values. It is common to refer to people by their first name, including co-workers and superiors. This reflects the country's emphasis on equality and creating a relaxed atmosphere.

4. Personal space:
Danes generally value personal space and tend to keep their distance in conversation. It is advisable to keep an appropriate distance, especially with strangers.

5. Hygge:
Hygge is a concept deeply rooted in Danish culture, referring to a cozy and warm atmosphere that creates a sense of comfort and contentment. Danes love to create a hygge atmosphere at home, in cafes, at social gatherings, and more. Make this concept your own by relaxing and having intimate conversations, enjoying good food and drink, and maintaining a cozy atmosphere.

1. Table manners:

When dining out in Denmark, it is customary to wait until everyone is seated before eating. Keep your hands visible on the table and use utensils properly. It is polite to chew with your mouth closed and avoid talking with food in your mouth.

2. Cheers and skål

Cheers are common at social gatherings, especially on special occasions. The Danish word for cheering is 'skål'. Raise your glass, make eye contact, and say "squall" before taking a sip. When toasting, it is polite to toast with everyone at the table.

3. Share food:
In some Danish dining rooms (such as family or informal gatherings) food is often served in the center of the table and guests serve their own. When serving food, care should be taken to eat in moderation so that there is enough for everyone.

4. Tipping
In Denmark, a service charge is usually included in the bill so tipping is not obligatory. However, we would appreciate it if you would leave a small tip as a thank you for the excellent service.
Festivals and celebrations:

1. Midsummer Night (Sankt. Hans Aften):
Midsummer is celebrated on the night of June 23rd and marks the beginning of summer in Denmark. Bonfires are lit and people gather to enjoy music, food, and socializing. The event often includes speeches, singing traditional songs, and burning dolls.

2. Christmas:
Christmas is an important celebration in Denmark. Danish Christmas traditions include decorating the Christmas tree, exchanging gifts, and enjoying a festive meal with family and friends. On Christmas Eve, many Danes attend church services and partake in a traditional Danish Christmas dinner that includes dishes such as roast duck or pork,

caramelized potatoes, red cabbage, and rice pudding. 3. New Year's Eve (Nytårsaften): New Year's Eve is celebrated with enthusiasm in Denmark. Many people gather with friends and family to welcome the New Year. Fireworks are a popular tradition and can be enjoyed as a breathtaking sight unfolding across the night sky. It is customary to enjoy celebratory meals and toast to the coming year with champagne or sparkling wine.

4. Danish Constitution Day (Grundlovsdag): Danish Constitution Day is celebrated on June 5th and commemorates the signing of the Danish Constitution in 1849. On this day Danes celebrate democracy and freedom.

Political speeches take place in public squares, providing an opportunity to reflect on national values and democratic principles.

5. Cultural Festival:
Denmark hosts a wide variety of cultural festivals throughout the year, including music, art, literature, and cinema. The aforementioned Roskilde Festival is one of Europe's largest music festivals. Aarhus Festival, Copenhagen Jazz Festival, and Copenhagen Cooking & Food Festival are other notable events celebrating Danish and international culture. 6. Birthdays and special occasions:
Danish birthdays are often celebrated with family and close friends.

It is customary to bring presents to the birthday boy and sing the Danish version of the happy birthday song called "Tillykke med fødselsdagen". Cakes and pastries are also common at birthday parties.

At these festivals and celebrations, it is polite to respect local customs and traditions. Danish society is generally relaxed and inclusive. Feel free to join the celebrations and join the conversation with the locals. Remember to greet people in a friendly way, keep an open mind and enjoy the unique cultural experiences Denmark has to offer.

Understanding and accepting Danish cultural etiquette and customs will enhance your interaction with the locals, deepen your appreciation of Danish culture and create an unforgettable experience during your stay in Denmark.

Chapter nine

*Practical Tips and Safety: Health and Safety
Precautions, Denmark Security for Visitors, Emergency
Contacts, Local Laws and Regulations, Tips for Solo
Travelers, Sustainable Travel Practices*

When traveling to Denmark, it is important to prioritize health and safety, understand local laws and regulations, and practice sustainable travel. This article provides practical tips and safety guidelines to ensure a smooth and comfortable stay during your visit to Denmark.

Health and safety precautions:

1. Health Insurance:
Before traveling to Denmark, it is recommended that you take out comprehensive travel health insurance to

cover the cost of emergency medical care. Make sure your insurance covers pre-existing conditions as well. 2. Vaccination:

Check with your doctor or travel clinic to see if any vaccinations are required before visiting Denmark. Routine immunizations such as measles, mumps, rubella, diphtheria, tetanus, and pertussis should be up to date.

3. Medical institutions:

Denmark has a well-developed healthcare system with modern medical equipment and highly qualified medical professionals. In the event of a medical emergency, dial the European emergency number 112 for immediate assistance.

4. Prescription drugs:

If you take prescription medication, make sure you have enough for the duration of your trip. We also recommend that you

carry a copy of your prescription or a letter from your doctor stating your medical need for the drug.

Safety for visitors to Denmark:

Denmark is generally considered a safe country for travelers. However, it is important to remain vigilant and take necessary precautions to ensure your safety.

1. Personal items:

Always keep personal belongings such as passports, wallets, and electronic devices safe. Avoid displaying valuables in public places and be careful in crowded areas where pickpockets can occur.

2. emergency contact:

Familiarize yourself with the Danish emergency numbers. In an emergency, dial

112 for police, fire brigade, and medical assistance.

3. Natural disasters:

Denmark has few natural disasters such as earthquakes and hurricanes.

However, it is advisable to check the local weather conditions as blizzards can affect transportation, especially in winter. Local laws and regulations:

1. Legal drinking age:
The legal drinking age in Denmark is 18. If you plan to drink alcohol, it is important to carry valid identification, such as a passport or driver's license.

2. Drug laws:
Denmark has strict drug laws and possession, use, and trafficking of illegal drugs is illegal and can lead to severe penalties. 3. Bicycle Rules:

Denmark is known for its bike-friendly culture. If you plan to ride a bicycle, familiarize yourself with local cycling rules. B. Use designated bike lanes, obey traffic lights, and wear a helmet when necessary.

Tips for solo travelers:

1. Safety precautions:

Denmark is generally safe for solo travelers, but sensible safety precautions are recommended. Avoid walking alone in secluded areas at night and let someone you trust know your itinerary and plans.

2. Local knowledge:

Soak up the friendly and hospitable character of the locals. Join the conversation to get recommendations and ask for advice on safe areas to explore, local customs, transportation options, and more.

3. Let's keep in touch:

Make sure you have a reliable means of communication. B. Access to a local SIM card or WiFi to stay connected with family, friends, or emergency services when needed. Sustainable travel practices:

Denmark is known for its commitment to sustainability and environmental protection. As a responsible traveler, you can contribute to these efforts by traveling sustainably.

1. Public transportation:

Denmark has an efficient and well-connected public transport system, including trains, buses, and bicycles. Choose public transport whenever possible to reduce your carbon footprint and minimize your environmental impact. Consider purchasing a resort (travel card) for convenient and environmentally friendly transportation.

3. Waste management:

Denmark focuses on waste management and recycling.

Please respect your local waste disposal system by sorting your rubbish into the appropriate recycling bins. Bring reusable water bottles and shopping bags to minimize single-use plastic waste.

Four. Energy saving:
Save energy by turning off lights, air conditioners, and other electrical appliances when not in use. Choose eco-friendly accommodation that prioritizes energy-efficient practices and sustainability.

5. Respect Nature and Wildlife:
Denmark has beautiful natural landscapes such as national parks, forests, and coastal areas. When visiting these areas, please follow designated trails, respect wildlife habitats, and avoid littering. Please be mindful of our sensitive ecosystem and

follow all applicable regulations and restrictions.

6. Support local sustainable businesses:
Choose accommodations, restaurants, and shops that prioritize sustainability and support local businesses. Look out for certifications such as Green Key, which shows your commitment to being environmentally friendly.

7. Reduce water consumption:
Denmark is known for its clean and abundant water resources, but it is still important to use water responsibly. To conserve water, keep showers short, turn off taps when not in use, and consider reusing towels and linens in hotels.

By adopting these sustainable travel practices, we can help preserve Denmark's natural beauty and support the country's commitment to environmental sustainability.

In conclusion, make health and safety your top priority when visiting Denmark by taking out travel insurance, following the necessary health precautions, and knowing your emergency contacts. Please respect local laws and regulations, be mindful of cultural etiquette, and take necessary precautions if traveling alone. Adopt sustainable travel habits by using public transport, biking or walking, managing waste, conserving energy and water, and supporting local sustainable businesses. If you act carefully and responsibly, you can have a safe, comfortable, and sustainable experience in Denmark.

Chapter ten

*Useful Phrases and Vocabulary: Basic Danish Phrases,
Numbers and Directions, Food and Drink Vocabulary*

Learning a few basic phrases and vocabulary when traveling in Denmark will greatly enhance your experience and make it easier to communicate with the locals. In this article, you'll find important Danish phrases, numbers, directions, and food and drink vocabulary to help you navigate your everyday life and get the most out of your trip.

Basic Danish Phrases:

1. Hello: Hej (Hey)

2. Good morning: Godmorgen (Goh-mor-n)

3. Good afternoon: God eftermiddag (Goh eh-ter-mee-dah)

4. Good evening: Godaften (Goh-ahf-ten)

5. Goodbye: Farvel (Fah-vel)

6. Thank you: Tak (Tahg)

7. Please: Vær så venlig (Vair so ven-lee)

8. Excuse me: Undskyld (Oons-kyld)

9. Yes: Ja (Ya)

10. No: Nej (Nay)

11. Sorry: Beklager (Beh-kla-er)

12. I don't understand: Jeg forstår ikke (Yai for-stop-eer ee-neh)

13. Do you speak English?: Taler du engelsk? (Tah-ler doo en-gelsk?)

14. Could you help me, please?: Kan du hjælpe mig, tak? (Kan doo yel-peh mai, tahg?)

15. Where is...?: Hvor er...? (Vor er...?)

16. How much does it cost?: Hvor meget koster det? (Vor met kost-er deht?)

Numbers and Directions:

1. Zero: Nul (Nool)
2. One: En (En)
3. Two: To (Toh)
4. Three: Tre (Tray)
5. Four: Fire (Fee-reh)
6. Five: Fem (Fem)
7. Six: Seks (Secks)
8. Seven: Syv (Suv)
9. Eight: Otte (Oh-teh)

10. Nine: Ni (Nee)

11. Ten: Ti (Tee)

12. Twenty: Tyve (Too-veh)

13. Thirty: Tredive (Tray-dee-veh)

14. Forty: Fyrre (Fur-reh)

15. Fifty: Halvtreds (Halv-treds)

16. Hundred: Hundrede (Hoon-dreh)

Directions:

1. Left: Venstre (Ven-streh)

2. Right: Højre (Hoy-reh)

3. Straight ahead: Ligeud (Lee-yeh-uhd)

4. Excuse me, where is the...?: Undskyld, hvor er...? (Oons-kyld, vor er...?)

5. Where is the nearest...?: Hvor er den nærmeste...? (Vor er den nair-mes-teh...?)

6. Can you show me the map?: Kan du vise mig på kortet? (Kan doo vee-seh mai poh kort-et?)

Food and Drink Vocabulary:

1. Breakfast: Morgenmad (Mor-gen-mad)
2. Lunch: Frokost (Froh-kost)
3. Dinner: Aftensmad (Af-tens-mad)
4. Water: Vand (Vahn)
5. Coffee: Kaffe (Kah-feh)
6. Tea: Te (Teh)
7. Beer: Øl (Ool)
8. Wine: Vin (Veen)
9. Bread: Brød
10. Cheese: Ost (Ost)

Meat: Kød (Kød)
Fish: Fisk (Fisk)
Chicken: Kylling (Kuh-ling)
Vegetables: Grøntsager (Grun-tsah-yer)

Fruits: Frugt (Frookt)

Salad: Salat (Sah-lat)

Soup: Suppe (Soo-peh)

Dessert: Dessert (Deh-sehr)

Bill, please: Regning, tak (Ren-ning, tahg)

Can I have the menu, please?: Kan jeg få menu, tak? (Kan yai for meh-noo-en, that?)

I am vegetarian: Jeg er vegetar (Yai er veh-geh-tar)

I have allergies: Jeg har allergies (Yai har al-ler-gee-er)

Cheers!: Skål! (Skawl)

Bon appétit!: Velbekomme! (Vel-beh-kom-eh)

Learning these basic Danish phrases, numbers, directions, and food and drink vocabulary will enable you to navigate everyday situations, interact with locals, and order food with ease. Danish people appreciate efforts to speak their language, even if it's just a few simple phrases, so don't hesitate to give it a try. Remember to approach conversations with a friendly attitude and be patient with yourself as you learn. Enjoy your time in Denmark and have fun exploring the language and culture!

Printed in Great Britain
by Amazon